YOUR BUDDY

A Childhood Journey

By

Chris Haley

Cyberwit.net
HIG 45 Kaushambi Kunj, Kalindipuram
Allahabad - 211011 (U.P.) India
http://www.cyberwit.net
Tel: +(91) 9415091004
E-mail: info@cyberwit.net

Printed at Vcore.

Dedicated to my Great Uncle Thomas "Buddy" Allen

You died young, so young you will always be.

I never met you, but I cherish your memory.

Photos courtesy of author

"Three Buddies" illustration by Alan Haley

Contents

Crib Baby

Standing,
my small arms
holding on to
wooden railings,
I jumped like a pogo stick.
Up and down,
up and down,
up and down,
I jumped until I fell asleep,
standing,
still supported by the rails.
My parents smiled remembering this.
I smile, too.
Now, my parents
and my crib are gone.
Or are all three together,
preserving each other in Heaven,
waiting to help their little boy
stand again?

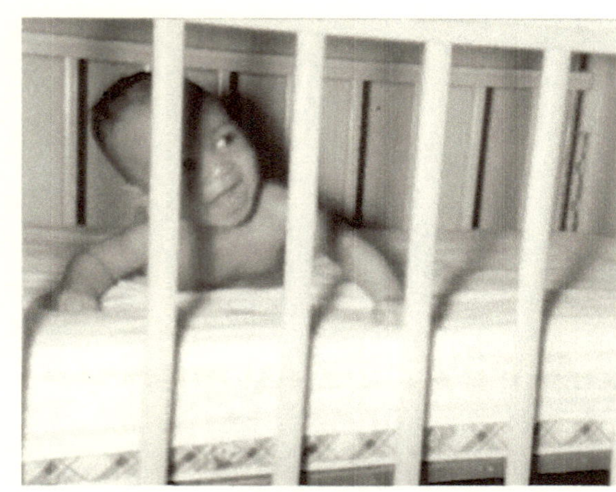

Nice Kids

I remember winters
when we stuck naked GI Joes
in water filled coffee cans,
so they'd freeze overnight
in action poses. I remember
summers at sunset when my
little friends and I excitedly
swung plastic bats, swatting
fireflies into the night, shattering
fluorescent body parts, counting
our innocent victims. We loved
this playtime. We never feared
scowling therapists might one day
diagnose our fun. We never feared
we weren't nice.

Pick Me

She had been picking on me
like she was better than me,
like she was smarter than me
and stronger than me.
Like because she was a girl
she could tease and say
whatever she wanted to me,
whatever she wanted at me.
I was a boy and she was a girl,
so I knew I was supposed to
let her be, but she pushed me
and pushed me and pushed me
and pushed me and pushed me,
SO I PUSHED HER BACK
and she stumbled back
onto the sidewalk. Crack!
The pavement pooled red
behind her little head,
more red than I'd ever seen.

She sprang up wailing.
Her arms pointed through pain.
Little feet raced through my porch
back door. Her mission had changed.
Her fists had stopped pounding me,
But I hurt worse than any
punch she had landed.
My stomach dropped
To the spot where she fell.

My lungs forgot
what breathing was.

I was so scared by what I'd done.
That I'd be perceived as mean
and a punk for pushing a girl,
even though she had started it.
I think I peed my pants on the way
to tell my mother and her mother,
who were inside playing cards,
Laughing,
what a monster I was.
But when the story was told,
my Mom boldly defended me
for defending me!
I've never forgotten being so
surprised at not getting whipped.
I wasn't a punk. I was Dee Haley's
little man who wouldn't allow a
bratty girl to pick on me.

Show and Tell

I held the book in my hand.
No, it wasn't a book, It was
a magazine. A Black magazine
written for a Black audience.
I sat on Mrs. Read's lap, my
fifth grade teacher, white,
chin length brown hair with
swoop bangs, bespectacled,
but probably younger than
my fifth grade mind imagined
a teacher could be. Patiently,
her strong, gentle hands comforted
me on her lap. I was shaking
as I reported on an article which
revealed President Abraham Lincoln's
words that he would be "damned if
the niggers is the first thing"
he'd have to deal with. Mrs. Read
cradled my sad, angry, percolating,
little body. Trembling, I said a hero
of mine had actually hated people
like me. My brown eyes teared up
and my small chest rat-a tat-tatted
like a drum. I hated knowing
what I knew. I feared telling my
30 classmates, whose fifth grade
attention challenged eyes glanced
back and forth, from complexions
and chairs as different and as similar

as an overloaded crayon box.
Maybe he was their hero, too.
I don't remember what Mrs. Read
or any of my classmates said.
I do remember I was a scared
little boy, who believed bringing
this story for show and tell
made me as brave as any
barrel chested man.

Two-Wheel Astronauts

We rode bikes like we were
astronauts soaring over the stars,
passing planet after planet,
never stopping to refuel,
because we were inexhaustible.
Until our parents yelled
"Come home!"
we would ride, wheelie, squeal, and
leave the darkest and slickest, sick
skid marks. On the street where I lived
my friends and I were unstoppable,
unnamed superheroes, who rode
on the wind like that's all
we were meant to do, cause
when you're kids, I know now,
you never think any of that
life
will stop.
When you grow up
you assume you'll still
ride bikes with your friends.
And sometimes, many years later,
If you're lucky,
you do.

For 15 years She Grinned

We visited the pound.
We walked down the row
of regulation sized crates and stalls.
The smell was alive, thick, sticky, and
reeked pet odors. Throughout the shelter,
yapping, barking, whining, and
the frantic slapping of tails against
cages and concrete walls echoed.
Older dogs and young puppies
fashed breathy tongues. Legs
flailed and paws stamped against
hard stained, soiled, ammonia rinsed
floors. German Shepherds, Collies,
and mixed breed mutts scampered,
creating a feverish animal kingdom
of playfulness, loneliness, and
desperation - this was not
a no-kill shelter. My slack face
knew these gasping, turning,
leaping Fidos had only days
to be saved.
Then we saw her, a brown
nosed, black torso,
smiling little fluff ball.
Her little lips flared
around little teeth,
smiling. My first pet. Our
darling, beaming, Peanut,
chose us and for 15 years,
we kept smiling.

A Bus Ride Named Desire

I wanted you
when I first saw you,
incredibly cute
standing next to your
best friend,
who I was taking
to the high school dance
that night. I wanted you
so badly. Soon, somehow,
we were in a play
and soon, somehow,
we became a thing,
and you were mine
to be had.
We rode together,
side by side,
on that fun trip,
in that sweet bus,
for that long ride.
We kissed and kissed.
I'd never mastered French
better than this.
But you were safe,
I was chaste,
because down below,
it was a no go.
I don't know why.
I absolutely wanted you!
My heart told me so.

My mind told me so.
But my body…no.

That's when I understood
why Davis, Garland, and Clift
were my heroes. That's when
my heterosexual dreams
let go.

My 25 Cents Worth!

Clanging pots and pans!

Twenty five cents,
That's all I wanted.

Waiters yelling out orders!

A quarter of a dollar
to show me I was
appreciated for being
The Family Fish House
Carryout Manager.

Cooks ringing bells that orders are ready!

Mindy, my manager, hesitated,
like somehow
twenty five cents
was too much too soon.

*Cash registers clinging open,
slamming closed!*

She had to "think about it."
At that moment, I decided
paper cones of fried fish

weren't worth my nineteen year old
dignity.

Different shifts punching time clocks!

I sure loved the fried shrimp though.

Swinging for the Stars

Standing alone
surrounded
by everyone,
but no one I knew,
because who was I
To know.
Just an eight year old kid
who signed up
for a community center's
talent show and sang
"Take Me Out To The Ballgame."
It seemed I sang to total

I don't remember anyone clapping
when I finished,
when my shot ended.

Still, I'll never forget
that moment
I went to bat,
swung,
struck out,
but was hooked.
I've been swinging ever since.

Fledgling Little Theatre Bitch

I stormed out of that auditorium
like I was the diva of diva's -
a Black boy's Patti LuPone and
a gay boy's Bette Davis who's
Spirit I claimed as my own.
My brain was baking at temperatures
I didn't know I could reach.
I was adolescent surliness
with an *All About Eve* mouth!
I stomped to the director's seat,
Blared, "You've lost all respect!"
and whirled around, temples
pounding, arms flailing,
my legs stabbing the floor,
As they stomped to a Tony
Award worthy, slamming doors,
auditorium exit! I overacted rage
for his casting someone else
in a role I didn't even want, while
I burned because he had given
The role I did want to a less
Talented senior who didn't
Share the acting dreams
I lived and breathed!
Catching my breath that night, I
Trembled in my bed and stained
My pillows with tears,
And wondered who I was.
I believed myself a talented,

Classic, golden age of cinema,
righteous bitch. But I really was
An immature, actors' biographies
reading whore, trying to fill
a part for which I was hardly ready,
but I wanted even more.
A star!

The Close-Up in *Meet John Doe*

His fingers trembled, alone,
on the television's black and white screen.
Painfully, I strained forward
In my school desk chair, transfixed.
I had never watched this movie,
so I had never studied this scene.
The small gesture
of his fidgeting phalanges
gripped me.
My thespian soul cried,
Cooper acting your fingers,
Capra directing this vision,
Barnes capturing that shot,
tell me how you created this?!
Burn in my being
the skill to travel this lane
and I'll sell my soul on the spot.

Do You Know Me?

When did it begin,
This fame fixation
Where all we want
Is to be wanted
By those we know
And don't know - the same.
When did we switch
From mind your business
To mining our personal business
For notoriety and riches
Without any hint of shame?
When did being a Kardasian
Become our 15 minute aim?

Innocent and Lovely

Our photo,
Back to back,
Shoulder to shoulder,
Hands clasped,
Unseen below the 3x5 frame.
You were Deedee to me,
I was Haley to you,
Like my parents' pet names.
Innocent and lovely in our beauty,
At my folks' celebration of 25 years,
Standing back to back,
Shoulder to shoulder
With each other,
We posed as a promising future pair.
Yet today, sweet Deedee,
Time has moved on
As we did.
And I don't recall
Your last name.

Touched in the Head

I sat across from my great grandma,
around the curve of the round,
chestnut brown, dinner table.
We had finished breakfast,
We were sitting and talking.
I loved being here, in Augusta,
in Georgia, in my great grandmother's
house. I loved the 16 ounce Pepsi bottles
and the hot chocolate sweet cups of
caffeinated, creamed-up coffee
she would let my brother and me drink
that our parents would never allow us
at our DC home. I loved playing
with the family dog, Boo,
who was older than me,
which I couldn't grasp,
but I loved him even more
because he was. I loved
my great grandmother,
Cooter Mama, funny name
and all. She loved us, too,
and cared for us every Christmas
and summer holiday which
we'd alway drive down in one day.
"We had to make it during daylight."
our father stressed, to see her
and our great granddaddy,
Daddy Hosea, and stay for two,
always two, wonderful weeks.

But this morning was different,
because Cooter Mama scrunched
her oval light toned face, and
looked at me, curiously. She asked
"Who is that woman?" sitting next
to her, at the curve in the round,
chestnut brown dinner table.
Cooter Mama asked who
that woman was? She asked
who that woman who was my mother
and her granddaughter was?
That's how, and that's where,
as an innocent, confused, little boy,
I was brutally introduced to
Alzheimer's.

Buddy

Strolling by your side,
It seemed like a movie,
the classic coming of age tale
where an elder and their charge
bond. One so proud, the other
so excited, because being together
meant we accepted, respected,
and loved each other. I felt protected
with you, Daddy Hosea,
my great grandpa, tall, lean, sturdy,
and funny. You cracked jokes
I'm sure a pre-adolescent boy
wasn't supposed to hear,
but my parents weren't here!
I was with you! We were
wicked pals at play! Two men
striding through the streets,
smiling, puffed out chests,
pausing at your neighbors' porches,
knocking at the church where
you served as a deacon, bragging
that I was your granddaughter,
Dolores' boy, your great grandson,
whom you called "Buddy".
"Buddy" whose white silhouetted face
lay centered in a stark black background
cutout, framed and hung in its cherished
spot over the fireplace. "Buddy".
Your son who had died as a child

years before my parents were
born. I loved being your new Buddy
as I settled into the barbershop chair,
surrounded by smelly tonics, buzzing
razors, and a country buffet of southern
fried stories. Waves of laughter, from
your animated grown friends warmed
and tickled me, even though I barely
understood anything that was said.
I never wanted to leave.
But we did.
A week later we went home.
Months later, we heard,
so did you.
Your Buddys miss you, Daddy Hosea.
Years from now, the three of us
will walk to the barbershop, again